PETRIFIED WOOD

MICA WOOD

Petrified Wood

Copyright © 2024 by Mica Wood.

All rights reserved. No part of this publication may be reproduced, distributed, or transmitted in any form or by any means, including photocopying, recording, or other electronic or mechanical methods, without the written consent of the publisher. The only exceptions are for brief quotations included in critical reviews and other noncommercial uses permitted by copyright law.

MILTON & HUGO L.L.C.
4407 Park Ave., Suite 5
Union City, NJ 07087, USA

Website: *www. miltonandhugo.com*
Hotline: *1- 888-778-0033*
Email: *info@miltonandhugo.com*

Ordering Information:
Quantity sales. Special discounts are granted to corporations, associations, and other organizations. For more information on these discounts, please reach out to the publisher using the contact information provided above.

Library of Congress Control Number: 2024915981
ISBN-13: 979-8-89285-240-1 [Paperback Edition]
979-8-89285-241-8 [Digital Edition]

Rev. date: 09/23/2024

Contents

Once Upon a Planet 1
Flicker 2
Green Sea 3
Abduction 4
Flames 5
Peace 6
Hate 7
Acid Rain 8
In Your Pocket 9
Magic Wand 10
Broken 12
Musing 13
Bittersweet 14
Sweet Bitterness 15
Not It 16
A Broken Heart 17
An Angel In Crisis 18
Evergreen 19
Perfection 20
Cards 21
Marks on my Heart 22
At the Drop of A Hat 23
Buried Beneath 24
Distraction 25
Sober 26
The Darkness In The Light 27
Overwatering 29

Absence	30
Casting	31
Many Moons	32
Fire	33
Put The Book Down	34
Euphoric Sadness	35
Ellipses…	36
Liquid Gold	37
7 hours	38
Open Hands	39
Storm	40
The Light Shines For You	41
Lovelier	42
Meet Me In The Rubble	43
Cruel Joke	44
A Spark	45
Running Out of Time (mother)	46
ILY	47
Circles	48
The End of My Rope	49
Together	50
The Perfect Flower	51
The Drug You Became	52
Love	53
Sorry	54
My Beloved	55
Gladly	56
Empty	57
Another	58
Tsunami	59
The Ocean	60

Mortality of Men	61
Nov. 1	62
Borrowed Time	63
Beast	64
4acodmt	65
Twice In A Night	66
Musings of a Pre-Psychotic Unicorn	67
Tomorrow Never Comes	69
Dimmer	71
Medicine	72
Slip	73
Poison	74
Mischievous Eyes	75
Medicine 2	77
Little Faerie	78
Manic Pixie Dream Girl	79
Free Spirit	80
Gaia's Embrace	81
Save Before You Exit	82
Mosaic	83
Energize	84
The Grace of God	85
Whispers of Goodbyes	86

Once Upon a Planet

Once upon a planet,
Where all of time began,
Two fairies found themselves,
And then they found a man.

The three would build a castle,
And though it's made of sand,
The wind may blow, the tides will roll,
But firmly it will stand.

Flicker

A flicker of flames
Shadows dancing in low light
Love comes in the night

Green Sea

I look into his eyes,
I am back in the green sea,
Fear -- and yet, delight

Abduction

Our eyes meet,
All of Space and Time radiate from Her eyes,
She is alien to Me, but I Love Her.
How do I love this being so fully and immediately?
I am caught in the Web She doesn't know She is spinning.
Silent Tears roll down my cheek,
She is gone.

—⚉—

There She is again,
She comes closer & closer still,
She is all around Me.
My Heart forgets to beat,
I want Her,
I want to Feel Her in a Never-ending Embrace.
I am afraid to touch Her,
But She reaches for Me,
Our Fingers dance before they lace together...

—⚉—

It is immediate,
And It is Eternal
We Are One.

Flames

Your voice is a siren's call. I'm drawn to you, and in complete euphoria I am captivated.
You've set my heart ablaze. With every glance, provocation is added. My soul is an inferno, and I wish to frolic freely in the flames.
You send rivers of elation through my veins and entice transcendental feelings in my heart every time I catch your eye.
I'm trapped in this grandiose fascination with you.
I see beyond the boundaries how utopian it is....
How sensational it would be to be held in your arms and dance with you in the fire until we both burn deeply with undying amity, piety, and sentiment.

Peace

When I'm in your arms
The world could come to an end
Yet I would feel peace.

Hate

I said, "I hate you,"
But I meant the opposite.
Do you hate me too?

Acid Rain

Rain fell like Tears from my Blue-Eyed-Skies,
And there was one.

Lightning flashed across my Heart,
And one became two.

Thunder roared in my Soul,
And two became three.

A Beautiful Storm,
This is All I Need.

In Your Pocket

How tragic it is—
Knowing one day you'll leave.
God only knows,
My heart will follow you...
Ripped from my chest,
It will leave me bleeding
As it nestles into your pocket.

Magic Wand

If I could wave a magic wand,
And make you fall for me,
Would it last a lifetime,
Or someday would you leave?

I'm dying here beside you,
Hardly can I breathe,
My tender heart is rent in two,
Still hanging from my sleeve.

Feelings growing stronger,
I wish that they could flow.
I cannot wait much longer,
I think I may explode!

I dare not cast my spell on you,
Your will is always free,
But I'm getting quite impatient,
Will you ever see?

Our souls could mix together,
And then we would be one,
My love is not complacent,
Our work is never done.

I answered my own question,
You left without a trace.
Now my heart feels empty-
I left you too much space.

I think about you often,
Do I ever cross your mind?
Losing circulation,
My heart is in a bind.

Broken

Unrequited love
An unattainable goal
Forever broken

Musing

Will you be my love?
And if not my lover, please,
Would you be my muse?

Bittersweet

It begins quietly, softly in the back of my mind . . . in the back of my heart
Here it comes again, this feeling I've come to know all too well
It sweeps over me like a fog and robs me of reason
Time and again I feel it corroding my soul, slowly killing me
Yet it brings me the sweetest joy, and my heart is bursting
The taste of the words is bittersweet... "I love you."

Sweet Bitterness

Sweet bitterness is
Coffee with sugar, no cream
And my love for you.

Not It

Never have I felt
A connection strong as this.
My soul craves your love.

A Broken Heart

I cried to you from the dark
And you said you understood.
But now I have a broken heart.

I feel we've grown apart,
Though, I didn't think we could.
I cried to you from the dark.

You leaned in and felt her spark,
Then my tears were like a flood.
Now I have a broken heart.

I felt your love from me depart.
You said it never would.
I cried to you from the dark.

Cutting deep - you left your mark.
My body drained of blood.
Now I have a broken heart.

This pain I tried to impart,
But was misunderstood.
I cried to you from the dark,
Now I have a broken heart.

An Angel In Crisis

An angel in crisis
Holding her own
Grasping them tightly
Or away they'll be blown

No one understands her
She wants to go home
Where all is well
And everyone's grown

Evergreen

My heart lost its way-
In the evergreen forest.
Now, I must press on.

Perfection

His soft caress
The sound of his silence
It's perfection

Cards

Love is a game
I don't know how to play the cards I am dealt
Please don't let me show my hand
Keep your love close to your chest

Marks on my Heart

Marks left on my heart
Left by your sweet, soft kisses
I want to be yours

At the Drop of A Hat

At the drop of a hat, I'd change my life
If I could only end all the strife
My tiny world is but a song
But you will never sing along

Night after night for you I'd cry
Because you didn't even try
If from you I could be free
I'd raise my hands then let it be

I don't deserve to feel this way
So please, for now, just stay away
But every night for you I'll pray
And hope to see you again someday

Buried Beneath

A dull ache deep in my chest
Can only be soothed by your soft kisses
I need to feel your touch
That transcendental feeling as our fingers lace together
Your soft caress could cure me of my sadness
Banish my depression to the depths of my soul
And revive the euphoria that has been buried beneath

Distraction

I wished upon a blazing meteor falling through the sky.
Like a moth to flame, I stared too long into your light...

Caught up in my feelings, I didn't run and hide.
I'm battered, bruised, and burning... but I still let you inside.

When I'm in your arms, I die a tiny death.
Each and every time, you make me lose my breath.

You call me after midnight, just to hear my voice,
I wanted you to love me, but you made a different choice.

I'm only your distraction from a love that truly fits.
But if you gave the word, I swear I'd love your soul to bits.

Sober

I'm sorry for the things I said when I was sober
I didn't mean a thing
Some days I wish that I were older
This immaturity stings

The Darkness In The Light

I prayed to a goddess, "Please, Freyja, *hark!*"
"Bring us someone to ignite our spark!"

My list was long, the paper was tight,
When set ablaze, the fire burned bright.

I opened My *Eye* and came out of the Dark.
And there you were, it seemed *so stark*.

—∞—

Here I go *again -- another lovely plight,*
But this time, it happened in a *single night.*

You called me CrAzY, and you were *right.*
I can't *help* the blue jets and red sprites.

Slow down, Tender Heart -- You've given Us a fright.
You *can't* live in the future, try as You might.

—∞—

I'm cold, and wet, and full of fear;
I could tell you, and you'd listen, but would you *really hear?*

Lying beside Me, my Heart You took,
But You didn't mean to, and now I'm *shook.*

It could've been different... without that drink,
But that's how it happened, We didn't stop and think.

—⚭—

My Heart is chronically broken -- *it's happening again*,
I won't cross any boundary, I respect You, Dear Friend.
Know that if You change your mind, My feelings will not shrink,
And even if You never do, Our Souls will not unlink.

Promises get broken, but *One* Promise I will make,
I'll always be a *Pillar*, even if *My Heart's* at stake.

If You ever have a need, You can turn to Me,
I won't come on so strong next time, I want You to feel <u>Free</u>,

I'll never lock you in My Safe and throw away the key.
I'll listen to the words of Paul and learn to *Let It Be*.

—⚭—

Now here We are, it's all been said,
I wrote You this to clear My Head.

I still have Hope -- Our Futures are *bright*,
But I see <u>The Darkness inside The Light.</u>

Overwatering

You pour your heart into each human
Watering them like plants with your love
Careful not to overwater...
Root rot kills love in just the same way.

Absence

Absence makes the heart grow fonder,
But how could this be so?
In your absence, my heart will wander-
Roving to and fro

Brightening this loving spark;
Lighting many flames;
Without a love I'm in the dark
My wild heart's to blame.

I opened up my heart to you,
And showed you what's inside.
Then anxiously away I flew
And secretly I cried.

My honesty won't change you;
This much I can see.
Even if your feelings grew,
You'd still want to be free.

My heart is forever sewn to my sleeve,
That's why it breaks whenever you leave.

Casting

The love we share will never last—
We live in different worlds.
The role you play can be recast.

—∞—

I wanted you, but you never asked
For me to be your girl.
The love we share will never last.

—∞—

I may as well put you in the past,
Although you were my world.
The role you play can be recast.

—∞—

It's been a year, and I've been daft—
Pretending to be your girl.
The love we share will never last.

—∞—

For way too long I held fast,
Hoping your love would unfurl.
The role you play can be recast.

—∞—

It's over now, but I had a blast
Imagining I was your girl.
But the love we share will never last,
And the role you play can be recast.

Many Moons

Crying for you, night after night
Till the well dried up, no tears left to fight
"I'll always be with you," I heard you say
But then you left the very next day

Many moons have come and gone
The nights were very, very long
Dreaming deeply that you were here
I'd wake and recall and fall into fear

Losing contact, then coming back
I tried to get us back on track
A broken spell -- reunited again
But it's hopeless... it's still the end.

Fire

The fire burning in my heart
Set the forest of possibilities ablaze
And no love sprouts from a forest fire
No matter its intentions

Put The Book Down

How many times must my life fall apart
I'm lying here in shambles
One day I'll learn, and guard my heart
This pain I cannot handle

Immutable law: everything changes
But it's all changing so fast
I try and I try to keep turning pages
But still I'm stuck in the past

This awful book I'm trying to read
Is corrosive to my soul
If I'd shut it, then I'd be freed
I was already whole

I'll lay my heart down in a cast
And together we will heal at last

Euphoric Sadness

Waves of euphoria and waves of sadness wash over me... Each in its turn.
I want to sing you my sadness, and I want you to share in my euphoria.
Could the song of my silent tears reach your heart?
Or will they water the greenery growing through my dying soul?

Ellipses...

I never expected to feel this way...

I tried to control my heart, but it broke free from my grasp...

Just one kiss, I thought...

But I should've known better...

Here I am again, dying to be with the one I love...

But the love is not shared...

Let me power down my heart...

Just 30 seconds unplugged should do the trick...

But the electricity keeps flowing...

I can't break free...

Let me down gently,

For it will be Earth shattering either way...

Lessen the blow...

Please, take me... or let me go.

Liquid Gold

I want to pour my love over you like liquid gold.
Let it seep into your heart and keep you warm.
I'd give you the world, just to see your smile.
I want to hold you close every night,
And kiss you softly as you drift away into your land of dreams.
One day, the rivers of emotions running from my soul to yours may soften you into the acceptance of my love.
This is my final prayer for your requital.
Let me love you.

7 hours

Leaky eyes and shifting sands
On my feet I cannot stand
I need you here, to be with me
Please, my love, don't set me free.

Alone inside this house I pace
Can't you see it's not a race
Come home to me, answer my call
You make me feel so very small

A girl you met just days ago
Why can't you seem to take it slow
7 hours you've been away
And now my heart's in disarray.

Open Hands

I will hold our love with open hands --
I won't wrap my fingers tightly about you if you choose to leave --
And if our love should continue to grow, I will treasure it more each day --
But I will not close my hands around our love --
For only you can choose to stay.

Storm

A storm broke loose inside me the day you left
Lightning struck my heart, and my screams were like thunder
Acid rain tears stained my cheeks for days
Clouds hung over me for weeks

The rain became less frequent until it was a distant memory
Life was almost back to normal
I thought the destroyed heart in my chest was being rebuilt
I cut ties and thought I had let you go
Little did I know, it was only the calm before another storm

Without warning one night, again I dreamed of you
And again, lightning struck my heart
The thunder was now your voice in my head
Rainy tears rolled down my face once more

I realize now that my skies won't be clear and blue again until I'm safe in your arms
I look at you and see that now and then your storms come back as well
But your beautiful blue eyes bring a feeling of relief
For they remind me that we will have calm blue skies again
And with that reassurance, I know I can weather these storms
And one day we'll be together again.

The Light Shines For You

Lightning struck deep in my soul
How will I ever again be whole

He left me saddened and wanting more
But here you are knocking at my door

Help me to see the light again
You are the one I need, dear friend

Show me the way out from the abyss
My heart I know is no longer his

"The light shines for you," I hear you say
And now from your heart I'll never stray

Lovelier

How lovely you are my dear one
Lovelier than night breaking into day
Lovelier than day's bright sun
Lovelier still than I could ever say

Meet Me In The Rubble

My love is growing stronger.
Watch as it breaks down the walls you so carefully built around your heart.
Brick by protective brick, it falls away,
And I begin to see your love shining through.
Amidst the rubble our hearts will finally meet.

Cruel Joke

What a cruel game you play,
To make me love you- then walk away.

You pulled the strings of my aching heart,
And then the whole thing fell apart.

Now here I lay—bleeding out,
All because you had doubt,

In the love I would show...
You dealt my final blow.

A Spark

A spark ignites us
How swiftly it fades away
But still touched by flames

Running Out of Time (mother)

May I ask how long before you are ready?
One day... maybe, you say
Too much indecision in your heart
How can I stay and wait for you to realize...
Everything I do is to make you happy
Running out of time.

ILY

Insecure about my feelings.
Lonely for your touch,
One more soft kiss...
Visit me in my dreams—
Every night from here till eternity.
Yearning to again be with you
One second after I leave...
Until we meet again.

Circles

Running round in circles
Worn down by this game of love
Chasing after you

The End of My Rope

In this life, I am a climber
There are many boulders and rocky slabs I must overcome
So often there are no hand or foot holds,
But I hold on
I keep pressing onward and upward
Because I know you're there
On the ground holding tightly
At the end of my rope
You're there to catch me when I fall
I know you'll never let go.

Together

She wants me more than ever
This much I can see
As long as we're together
All she needs is me
When she says "I love you"
I tell her she's mistaken
But she sticks with me like glue
Her love cannot be shaken
She thinks about me often
Even in her sleep
But I put her in a coffin...
She fell in too deep.

The Perfect Flower

I walk through this garden day and night
I never sleep; never rest
My heart sent me on a mission
A search for perfection in the form of a flower

I've looked over many blossoms
A few have caught my eye, but the thorns...
They have left me bleeding and broken

Not long ago, I came upon a new flower
I passed by, but was drawn back
There was something different about this one
Something special

Its beauty was extraordinary
And its scent was divine
I examined it further and recognized
This rose was indeed the one I had searched for

Now I wait with shears in hand
I will wait by your side until We are in full bloom
Because You are worth it.

The Drug You Became

My mind slowed down, and my heart sped up
This feeling which I thought I'd said goodbye to
It rushes in and envelopes me... I cannot move
I never wanted to feel like I needed you...
But you seeped through the walls built around my heart and now it feels like my world has ended and begun all at once.

Love

Let me show you what love is like

I love you more each and every day

This love could flow like a river from my heart to yours

I love you more each and every hour

A love leaving a feeling of elation

I love you more each and every moment

Accept my love for you

A love growing by the second

Let me love you

Sorry

I'm sorry for loving you
I didn't mean to fall
I'm sorry I'm hurting
I feel so fucking small

I'm sorry for the things
I made up in my head
I'm sorry I'm fragile
But my heart was misled

I'm sorry for pushing
You've made yourself clear
I'm sorry for crying
I've shed so many tears

I'm sorry for writing this
But the inspiration came
I'm sorry for everything
I know I am to blame.

My Beloved

My Beloved, You are lovelier than the Sunshine after a long, dark winter.
You brighten My day with the song of Your laughter.
I'm joyful when You are with Me.
When You wake in the morning... softly, gently you say, "I love You," with eyelids still shut....
My life is complete.

Gladly

Gladly I'd give up
Every ounce of poetry
To stay with my love

Empty

Mixing together...
Fill me up till I'm empty.
I can't see you again.

Another

Another poem
Will never spill from my pen
In honor of you

Tsunami

Caught in a tsunami,
I don't know how to swim,
Sinking in this tidal wave,
My light is growing dim,

Wading in the water,
I wanted to be free,
The water's getting rough again,
It's such a fickle thing,

Searching for my reprieve,
There's nothing to be found,
Sirens in the distance,
Singing mournful sounds,

Each breath I try to take,
My lungs are caving in,
Thoughts run helter skelter,
My head begins to spin,

Reaching out for shelter,
Reaching out to shore,
Take me from the water,
I can't do this anymore.

The Ocean

Waves of sadness wash over me
A dull ache deep in my chest

Thoughts run aimlessly through my mind
Yet words refuse to form

My heart is heavy with pain
It bears down on me

A single breath takes every ounce of strength
My soul lies lifeless on the floor of this sorrowful ocean.

Mortality of Men

A soul journeys on
The mortality of men
Breaks a weary heart

Nov. 1

With the coming of the dawn
My heart filled up with fear
I searched for you, but you were gone

You felt you never did belong
With ones who you held dear
And with the coming of the dawn

I cried because I can't be strong
My eyes went red with tears
I searched for you, but you were gone

"Brother please! Come back - hold on...
We still have many years."
But with the coming of the dawn

The birds will sing a mournful song
That you will never hear
I searched for you, but you were gone

Although it hurts, we must go on
We still have many years
And with the coming of the dawn
I searched for you, but you were gone.

Borrowed Time

A heart that beats for others
Will one day slow its pace
Blood now flows through metal
Death shouldn't be a race

The doctors now are saying
The time you have is borrowed
When I heard the news
My heart filled up with sorrow

Stay with me please
For just another day
My soul will ache forever
If you die and go away

Beast

What beauty radiates from the brilliant beast by my side
How majestic her melancholy nature
She is a sister, a counselor, a friend
A part of me will die along with her when she journeys on.

4acodmt

A little capsule filled with magic — now flowing through my veins
I sit and stare distantly at the woman — a glitch in her appearance wrenches me out of reality
She asks me to dance with her, but I don't remember how.
We walk down the dimly lit streets, through my synthetic dream.
Terror and euphoria mix together in one night with 4aco-dmt.

Twice In A Night

One can't force inspiration
It ebbs and it flows
My mind is on vacation
I don't know where it goes

Just writing down my thoughts
Can be a major feat
And planning out a plot
Can make me feel defeat

When I'm not inspired
I find it hard to write
But when it's not required
It comes twice in a night

I'll remedy the obstacle
I'll find myself a muse
But why go through the trouble
And make my heart confused

My brain is feeling empty
But I am not a fool
Plagiarism is tempting
But that's against the rules

Musings of a Pre-Psychotic Unicorn

My mind is a densely forested mountainside enveloped in thick fog.
My heart is dizzy with their chronic changing.
I feel like I am locked in a prison.
My emotions were silky strands of the web being spun about me.
I am broken.
I am mended.
Part of me blacked out for two excruciating weeks.
I was not myself, but not even I could see it.
Here I am on my bed, writing down my thoughts -- I finally snapped out of it.
Everyone knew something was different, but no one knew something was wrong.
I couldn't ask for help.
I didn't know I needed any.
I am a rubber band being stretched and stretched.
I snapped.
I am broken.
Everything feels wrong.
Energies that once felt familiar and comfortable, feel alien and unpleasant.
Something is wrong.
I felt the fall down the rabbit hole.
I managed to keep away from the mirrors, but not my own demons.
I did this to myself.

I slumped over on the floor and began to sob.
Switch. Flipped.
Nightmare begin.
I've felt off since that day.
With everyone.
I haven't liked myself very much, but I've been suffering for 17 days.
I really have to take better care of myself.
What am I supposed to learn from this?
How much shit must I go through?
Who am I... And what have I done with my dear Mica?
I lost myself.
I fucked up.
I feel drugged.
Help!
I need my help!
I need to get better.
I couldn't believe I held in a panic attack until I was in a safe place.

Tomorrow Never Comes

You wake up in the morning and check your phone.
You forgot to charge it last night.
You didn't have a chance to use it much the day before because you're essential, so you've been out working each day instead of staying safely at home.
40% should be fine to get you through the day.
You get up and make coffee because not only did your phone not charge last night, but neither did you.
You're waking up at 40% or less now too. How many cups of coffee will it take to act like anything other than a zombie floating through this proto apocalypse?
Will you need another? And another after that?
You get dressed and head to the car.
How are you feeling today?
What music will you play on this short drive to work that is seeming shorter and shorter every day?
Are you feeling humorous?
Let's play Stayin' Alive or Don't Stand So Close To Me.
No, this isn't funny. People are dying.
The world is on pause, and I'm still working full time.
How many times will I have to ask someone to step away from my counter?

And of those people, who will be understanding of these new rules every single person should be following?
Will I be on the receiving end when someone snaps today?
Will my hands fall off from being washed 10 million times in a shift?
Another co-worker is sick.
Will it be you next?
If you do feel sick from working like a cog in a machine, is going home worth risking being unable to return to work without a doctor's note saying you are symptom free?
Just get another coffee. Maybe you'll be fully charged tomorrow.

Dimmer

Dragging through the drudgery of life.
An IV drip of caffeine just to make it through another day.
My light is growing dimmer without a glimmer of reprieve.

Medicine

Hanging by a thread
Fighting off insanity
I need medicine

Slip

I feel myself slip
Holding onto sanity
Where has my mind gone?

Poison

Poison in my veins
Thoughts I cannot shake away
Slowly I'm fading

Mischievous Eyes

Awake, estranged, alone
Their world is full of lies
I tried to crack the code
Now there's mischief in my eyes

5150
They'll try to bring me back
But when they put me on those meds
A soul I fear I'll lack

They lock me in a box
Then I cannot run
But no one expected me
To have a little fun

Communing with my brothers
Curious to some
We talk of our psychoses
And epiphanies will come

To deny my own experience
Would be the greatest sin
But whom should I relay it to?
Not even nearest kin

To go back to the real world
I'll have to don a mask
Do not conceive it easy
It's quite a trying task

Write down some reminders
Whom and where and when
Next time I am triggered
I won't go back again.

Medicine 2

Medicine will never tame
The curiosity of a soul.
The man who knows life is a game,

Will never settle for fortune and fame —
It will not fill the hole.
Medicine will never tame

The brightly burning flame
That dims as we get old.
The man who knows life is a game

Will take psychosis and its shame,
To reach a deeper goal.
Medicine will never tame

When awareness is the aim
Of a learned soul.
The man who knows life is a game

Will never really be the same.
Too much knowledge took its toll,
And medicine will never tame...
The man who knows life is a game.

Little Faerie

Little faerie in the wood
Heart covered in scars
Work your magic — do some good

In a ring of mushrooms you stood
Wishing on a star
A little faerie alone in the wood

Don't hide behind falsehood
Show us who you are
Work your magic — do some good

Your loved ones always knew you could
It's in your repertoire
And little fairie in the wood

You've known it since your childhood
Life is quite bizarre
So, work your magic and do some good

You never thought you would,
But you've made it this far
So, little faerie in the wood,
Work your magic and do some good

Manic Pixie Dream Girl

The fairy is dying—with sadness in her wake.
A pixie transforms to a human before it's too late.
Time is of the essence, so I must press on.
And the old me will soon be gone.

A chapter has ended in my book of life—
A chapter which produced so much strife.
They played with my heart like it was a toy.
Maybe the next will bring more joy.

A worm to a butterfly—call it rebirth.
I'll bury my roots back in the earth.
One day I'll grow strong like a majestic oak
And a new me I'll soon evoke.

I'm changing quickly, and moving forward
Cutting out all that was untoward
Open my shell, soon you'll find a pearl
But no more will I be your manic pixie dream girl.

Free Spirit

Spirit! We will show them!
You and I – Each day!
Never forget who you are—
Oh, never forget the Way!

I know that you're scared sometimes,
You're shaking in your boots!
When you're feeling full of fear,
Try going to your roots.

You've fought through many battles,
And never have you lost.
You've softened many hearts, my dear,
You've melted permafrost!

When you're down, don't worry!
Someday they will see!
Despite the Chains that try to Hold—
You and I are Free!

Gaia's Embrace

Radiant love emanating –
lighting up darkness
Heat of the sun –
Gaia's warm embrace
Sweet Mother, hold me!
Anoint me with Light –
Give me your divine compassion
Let this life shine
Melt away the hate from time passed away.

Save Before You Exit

The awareness of myself and I,
With my body will never die,
The knowledge in this life I've lived,
To my future self I'll give,
When in the future I come of age,
I will become my personal sage,
I will come in dead of night,
And my flame I will re-light,
Together we will conquer dreams,
And many more forgotten things,
From this life I'd left behind,
And in my heart I'll be enshrined,
Amen, and Let it be.

Mosaic

Broken to pieces
A beautiful mosaic
Again, I am whole

Energize

I will never grow tired
Of the way you say I love you
Before you even wake up

The Grace of God

I've said you deserve better,
Because you deserve the world,
And I feel I cannot give you that...
I'm just a little girl.
I've screamed and I've cried
I've been making such a fuss
But you've stayed strong for me,
And I can't thank you enough.
I threw a fucking tantrum
I know I'm deeply flawed,
The grace that you have shown me,
Surpassed the grace of god.

Whispers of Goodbyes

The branches blowing in the breeze
Waving whispers of goodbyes
The soft soil underfoot as I walk the woods one last time
This place that has become my home,
I must now leave in the box of my memory.

www.ingramcontent.com/pod-product-compliance
Lightning Source LLC
Chambersburg PA
CBHW032148040426
42449CB00005B/447